Katherine HENGEL

Cool
BASIL

from
Garden to Table

How to Plant, Grow, and Prepare Basil

A Division of ABDO

ABDO
Publishing Company

visit us at www.abdopublishing.com

Published by ABDO Publishing Company, a division of ABDO, P.O. Box 398166, Minneapolis, Minnesota 55439. Copyright © 2012 by Abdo Consulting Group, Inc. International copyrights reserved in all countries. No part of this book may be reproduced in any form without written permission from the publisher. Checkerboard Library™ is a trademark and logo of ABDO Publishing Company.

Printed in the United States of America, North Mankato, Minnesota
102011
012012

 PRINTED ON RECYCLED PAPER

Design and Production: Anders Hanson, Mighty Media, Inc.
Series Editor: Liz Salzmann
Photo Credits: Aaron DeYoe, Shutterstock. Photos on page 5 courtesy of W. Atlee Burpee & Co.

The following manufacturers/names appearing in this book are trademarks: Kraft®, Kemps®, Market Pantry®, Pam®, A Taste of Thai®, Crystal Sugar®, Land O'Lakes®, Michael Graves Design®, Pyrex®, The Pampered Chef®, Proctor Silex®, Kitchen Aid®

Library of Congress Cataloging-in-Publication Data
Hengel, Katherine.
 Cool basil from garden to table : how to plant, grow, and prepare basil / Katherine Hengel.
    p. cm. -- (Cool garden to table)
 Includes index.
 ISBN 978-1-61783-182-9
 1. Basil--Juvenile literature. 2. Cooking (Basil)--Juvenile literature. I. Title.
 SB303.B37H46 2012
 583'.96--dc23
                    2011036623

Safety First!

Some recipes call for activities or ingredients that require caution. If you see these symbols, ask an adult for help!

Sharp - You need to use a sharp knife or cutting tool for this recipe.

Hot - This recipe requires handling hot objects. Always use oven mitts when holding hot pans.

Nuts - This recipe includes nuts. People with nut allergies should not eat it.

CONTENTS

WHY GROW YOUR OWN FOOD?

Because then you get to eat it, of course! You might not be the biggest basil fan in the world. But have you ever had fresh basil? Straight from your very own garden? If not, prepare to be surprised. Fresh food tastes wonderful!

Plus, fresh food is really healthy. All produce is good for you. But produce that comes from your own garden is the very best. Most folks do not use chemicals in their home gardens. That makes home gardens better for you and the **environment**!

Growing your own food is rewarding. All it takes is time, patience, soil, water, and sunshine! This book will teach you how to grow basil in **containers**. Once it's ready, we're going to use it in some tasty recipes!

BASIL

Basil is a tender **herb** that grows low to the ground. It originated in India and Iran. It has been around for thousands of years.

There are several kinds of basil. Italian dishes often call for sweet basil. Thai basil, lemon basil, and holy basil are frequently used in Asian dishes. Basil's flavor changes when it is cooked. So it is usually used fresh.

In this book, we're going to grow and cook sweet basil! Sweet basil grows very well in **containers**. Plus, you can use it in many different kinds of recipes. Let's get started!

TYPES OF BASIL

LEMON BASIL   **GREEK BASIL**   **HOLY BASIL**   **SWEET BASIL**   **THAI BASIL**

GROWING

In this book, you'll learn how to grow basil in a **container** garden. With container gardens, you have more control over things such as light and temperature. But keep in mind that basil grows differently in every climate.

When to Plant

Go online to find out the average date of the last frost in your area. Plant your seeds about three weeks after this date.

The Right Conditions

Sunlight
Basil is native to some of the warmest places on earth! It loves full sun for six to eight hours a day.

Temperature
*Basil seeds **germinate** at 70 to 75 **degrees**. Keep basil plants inside until temperatures are above 50 degrees at night.*

The Right Soil
Basil likes rich, warm soil that drains well.

SEEDS

1

2

3

MATERIALS NEEDED

12-inch wide container with drainage holes

soil

water

basil seeds

spray bottle

trowel

(1) Fill the **container** three-quarters full of soil. Wet the soil thoroughly. Sprinkle a few seeds on top. Space the seeds about 2 inches (5 cm) apart.

(2) Cover the seeds with ¼ inch (.6 cm) of soil.

Wet the soil using the spray bottle. Then place the container in a warm spot with full sun.

(3) Spray the soil often to keep it moist until the seeds **sprout**.

STAGES OF

Watering

The soil should be evenly moist, but not too wet. Water the plants in the morning. Put the water at the base of the plant, not on the leaves. Let the soil dry out a little between watering.

Thinning

Thinning means getting rid of a few basil **sprouts** so others have room to grow. When the sprouts are two inches tall, thin them. Each plant needs at least six inches of space. You can plant the ones you remove in another **container**.

WATER your basil plant in the morning. Be sure to water near the soil and not on the leaves.

THIN the sprouts when they are 2 inches (5 cm) tall.

GROWTH

Pinching

When a plant is 6 inches (15 cm) tall, pinch off the main stem directly above the third set of leaves. As the plant grows, do this for each branch. If flowers appear, pinch them off right away. You can use the leaves you pinch off in cooking.

Harvesting

Harvest the basil before autumn. After that, it will start growing flowers and stop making new leaves. The basil will also not taste very good. To harvest, cut or pinch off the stem.

PINCH off the stem above the third set of leaves. Do this every couple of weeks.

HARVEST your basil before autumn.

9

HARVESTING

BASIL

①

②

③

④

① Harvesting basil is as simple as pinching. Always pinch off the stem right above a set of leaves.

② Place the harvested stems in water. This keeps it fresh for a few days.

③ Or you can remove the stems and put the leaves in a plastic zipper bag. Store it in the refrigerator.

④ Before using, clean the basil in a bowl of cool water. Blot it dry.

How long will it take to grow?

It depends on the sun, temperature, and type of basil. Most plants **mature** within 60 to 90 days.

My basil looks good, but it doesn't taste very good!

It may have been given too much **fertilizer**. This causes the plant to grow quickly, without **developing** the oils needed for flavor. Basil flavor can also be ruined by allowing flowers to grow on the plant or harvesting it too late.

Why are there black spots on the leaves?

Bacteria causes these spots. It happens when soil splashes up on the leaves. Prevent these spots by watering near the base of your plant.

Why are my leaves yellow and wilted?

The plant probably has a plant sickness called fusarium wilt. It's caused by a **fungus**. You will have to start over with new soil and new seeds.

Cool Ingredients

6-INCH PITAS

AMERICAN CHEESE

BAKING POWDER

BREAD

BUTTER

BUTTERMILK

CAKE FLOUR

CANNED TOMATOES

CASHEWS

CAYENNE PEPPER

CHICKEN BROTH

COOKING SPRAY

EGGS

FISH SAUCE

GARLIC

LEMONS

BASIL PESTO

To make your own basil pesto sauce, loosely chop 2 cups of fresh basil leaves, ⅓ cup pine nuts, and 3 garlic cloves. Put them in a blender with ½ cup grated Parmesan, ½ cup olive oil, and salt and pepper to taste. Use the pulse setting until the mixture is smooth. Stop frequently to scrape the sides with a rubber spatula.

LIMES

MIXED BERRIES

MOZZARELLA CHEESE

OLIVE OIL

PARMESAN CHEESE

PIZZA CRUST

PROVOLONE CHEESE

RICE NOODLES

SALT AND PEPPER

SOUR CREAM

SUGAR

TOMATO JUICE

TOMATOES

VANILLA EXTRACT

VEGETABLE OIL

WHIPPING CREAM

Kitchen Tools

9-INCH SPRINGFORM PAN

BAKING SHEET

BASTING BRUSH

BLENDER

DINNER KNIFE

CUTTING BOARD

HAND MIXER

GARLIC PRESS

LARGE POT

MEASURING CUPS

MEASURING SPOONS

MIXING BOWLS

*Basil is an annual **herb**. It is in the mint family. In addition to being used in cooking, basil has also been used in perfumes, soaps, **shampoos**, and **dental** preparations!*

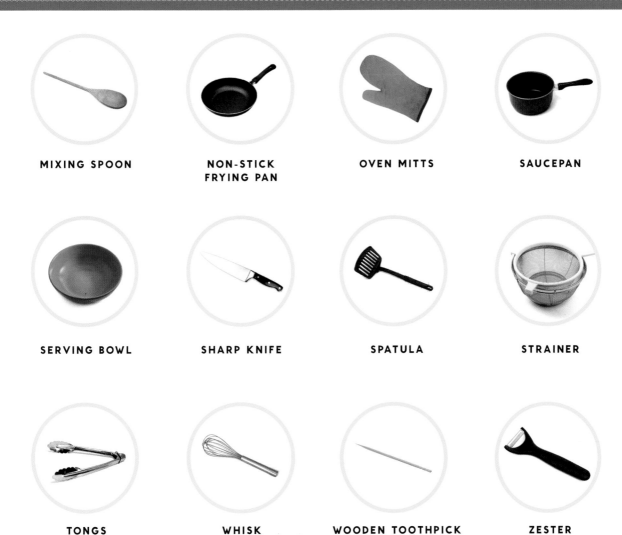

MIXING SPOON

NON-STICK
FRYING PAN

OVEN MITTS

SAUCEPAN

SERVING BOWL

SHARP KNIFE

SPATULA

STRAINER

TONGS

WHISK

WOODEN TOOTHPICK

ZESTER

Cooking Terms

Beat

Beat means to mix well using a whisk or electric mixer.

Chop

Chop means to cut into small pieces.

Grease

Grease means to coat something with butter or oil.

Julienne

Julienne means to slice into very thin strips.

Press

Press means to push an ingredient, often garlic through a garlic press.

Spread

Spread means to make a smooth layer with a spoon, knife, or spatula.

Stir-Fry

Stir-fry means to fry quickly over high heat in an oiled pan while stirring continuously.

Toss

Toss means to turn ingredients over to coat them with seasonings.

Whisk

Whisk means to beat quickly by hand with a whisk or a fork.

Zest

Zest means to lightly remove some of the peel from a **citrus** fruit using a zester.

BIG-TIME
Basil Parmesan Dip

Serve this creamy dip with oven-fresh pita chips!

MAKES 8 SERVINGS

INGREDIENTS

4 6-inch pitas

cooking spray

¼ teaspoon salt

½ teaspoon pepper

1 cup lightly packed
fresh basil leaves

¾ cup grated
Parmesan cheese

¾ cup reduced-fat
sour cream

2 teaspoons fresh
lemon juice

1 garlic clove, pressed

TOOLS

sharp knife

cutting board

baking sheet

measuring spoons

oven mitts

measuring cups

garlic press

blender

serving bowl

① Preheat the oven to 375 **degrees**. Split the pitas in half. Cut each half into eight wedges.

② Coat the baking sheet with cooking spray. Put the pita wedges on the baking sheet. Spray them lightly with cooking spray. Sprinkle them with salt and ¼ teaspoon pepper. Bake for 12 minutes or until crisp.

③ Put the basil, cheese, sour cream, lemon juice, garlic, and ¼ teaspoon pepper in a blender. Blend until smooth.

④ Pour the dip into a serving bowl. Serve with the warm pita chips.

Even Cooler
In a hurry? Instead of making your own pita chips, buy a bag at the store.

1

2

3
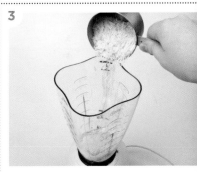

4

PERFECT

Pizza Margherita

This classic pizza is fit for (and named after) a queen!

MAKES A 12-INCH PIZZA

INGREDIENTS

½ pound tomatoes, chopped

1 clove garlic, pressed

½ teaspoon salt

olive oil

12-inch prepared, uncooked pizza crust

6 ounces mozzarella cheese, grated

6 fresh basil leaves, julienned

¼ cup grated Parmesan cheese

TOOLS

measuring spoons

sharp knife

cutting board

garlic press

mixing bowl

mixing spoon

baking sheet

basting brush

measuring cups

oven mitts

1. Preheat the oven to 500 **degrees**. Combine the tomatoes, garlic, salt, and 2 tablespoons olive oil in a mixing bowl. Set it aside.

2. Put the pizza crust on a baking sheet. Brush it lightly with olive oil. Top the crust with the mozzarella cheese. Then add the tomato mixture. **Drizzle** olive oil over the pizza.

3. Bake for 8 to 10 minutes, until the crust is golden brown and the cheese is bubbly. Remove it from the oven. Sprinkle the Parmesan cheese and basil over the top.

4. Let the pizza cool for 2 to 3 minutes. Cut it into wedges.

Did You Know?

Italian chef Raffaele Esposito of Naples created Margherita pizza in 1889 in honor of Queen Margherita.

1

2

3

Tomato Basil Soup

This amazing soup hits the spot any day!

MAKES ABOUT 4 SERVINGS

INGREDIENTS

26 ounces canned
tomatoes

2 cups tomato juice

1 cup chicken broth

¼ cup loosely packed
fresh basil

1 cup whipping cream

2 tablespoons butter

Salt and pepper

TOOLS

measuring cup

blender

can opener

saucepan

mixing spoon

oven mitts

serving bowls

(1) Put the tomatoes, tomato juice, and chicken broth in a saucepan. Bring it to a boil. Let it simmer for 20 minutes.

(2) Carefully pour the tomato mixture into a blender. Add the basil. Blend until smooth.

(3) Return the blended mixture to the saucepan. Turn the heat on low. Mix in the cream and butter until melted. Add salt and pepper to taste.

4 Put the soup in serving bowls. **Garnish** each bowl with a few basil leaves. Serve warm.

1

2

3

23

TASTY
Thai Noodles & Basil

This easy classic is oh, so light and delicious!

24

MAKES 2 TO 4 SERVINGS

INGREDIENTS

8 ounces rice noodles

1 cup fresh basil,

½ cup chopped cashews

3 garlic cloves

¼ cup olive oil

1 tablespoon fresh lime juice

1 tablespoon fish sauce

½ teaspoon cayenne pepper

2 tablespoons vegetable oil

TOOLS

large pot

oven mitts

strainer

measuring cups

measuring spoons

blender

non-stick frying pan

tongs

mixing spoon

① Bring a large pot of water to a boil. Remove from heat and add the noodles. Let them soak about 10 minutes until they are soft but still crunchy. Strain the noodles and rinse them with cold water. Set the noodles aside.

② Put half the basil and half the cashews in a blender. Add the garlic, olive oil, lime juice, fish sauce, and cayenne pepper. Blend until smooth.

③ Heat a large frying pan over medium-high heat. Coat it with the vegetable oil. Add the noodles. Gently turn the noodles with tongs. Stir-fry for 1 minute.

④ Put some of the basil mixture in the pan. Continue stir-frying for a couple of minutes, until the noodles are soft.

5 Remove from heat. Add the remaining basil mixture and fresh basil. Toss well. Sprinkle the remaining cashews on top.

Cheese & Pesto Sammy

One taste, and you'll forget regular grilled cheese!

MAKES 1 SANDWICH

INGREDIENTS

2 slices bread

1 tablespoon butter

1 tablespoon prepared pesto (see page 13)

1 slice provolone cheese

2 slices tomato

1 slice American cheese

TOOLS

non-stick frying pan

dinner knife

measuring spoons

spatula

sharp knife

cutting board

oven mitts

1. Heat a non-stick frying pan over medium heat. Butter one side of a bread slice. Place the slice buttered side down in the pan. Spread ½ tablespoon pesto on the bread slice.

2. Place the provolone cheese, tomato slices, and American cheese on top.

3. Spread the remaining pesto on one side of the second slice of bread. Place the slice pesto side down onto the **sandwich**. Butter the top of the sandwich.

4. When the bottom of the sandwich is golden brown, flip it over. Fry it until the second side is golden brown. Remove the sandwich from the pan. Cut it in half.

1

2

3

4

27

BEAUTEOUS
Basil-Lemon Cake

Who knew basil could be so great in a cake?

INGREDIENTS

2½ cups cake flour

2½ teaspoons baking powder

½ teaspoon salt

½ cup butter, softened

1½ cups sugar

2 large eggs, beaten

½ cup chopped fresh basil

2 tablespoons lemon zest

1 teaspoon vanilla extract

1 cup plus 2 tablespoons buttermilk

1½ cups mixed berries

TOOLS

9-inch springform pan

measuring cups

measuring spoons

mixing bowls

oven mitts

whisk

hand mixer

zester

sharp knife

cutting board

wooden toothpicks

1   Preheat the oven to 375 **degrees**. Lightly grease the springform pan.

2   Whisk the flour, baking powder, and salt together in a medium bowl. Set it aside.

3   Put the butter and sugar in a large bowl. Beat on medium speed until creamy. Add the eggs, basil, lemon zest, and vanilla extract. Beat until smooth.

4   Add one-third of the dry mixture to the wet mixture. Beat on low speed until smooth. Add one-third of the buttermilk. Beat until smooth. Repeat, **alternating** between adding dry mixture and buttermilk.

5   Pour the batter into the springform pan. Bake for 35 to 45 minutes, or until a toothpick stuck in the center comes out clean. Let the cake cool for 10 minutes. Remove the sides of the pan. Let the cake cool completely. Cut into wedges. Serve with berries.

2

3

4

5

WRAP IT UP!

Did you enjoy growing food from the earth? Are you a gifted cook with fresh ingredients? Fresh ingredients go a long way toward making food taste great. Ask the best chefs in the world. They'll tell you! Fresh ingredients are their secret ingredients!

By now you know that fresh food tastes great. Plus, it's good for the **environment**. Food from your garden doesn't require **transportation** or packaging. It isn't covered in harmful chemicals either!

So keep at it. Don't lose that green thumb! Think about your favorite foods. Can you grow them yourself? Chances are, you can. Check out the other books in this series. There may be a book about growing and cooking your favorite food!

Glossary

ALTERNATE – to change back and forth from one to the other.

CITRUS – a fruit such as an orange, lemon, or lime that has a thick skin and a juicy pulp.

CONTAINER – something that other things can be put into.

DEGREE – the unit used to measure temperature.

DENTAL – having to do with teeth.

DEVELOP – to grow or change over time.

DRIZZLE – to pour in a thin stream.

ENVIRONMENT – nature and everything in it, such as the land, sea, and air.

FERTILIZER – something used to make plants grow better in soil.

FUNGUS – an organism, such as mold or mildew, that grows on rotting plants.

GARNISH – to decorate with small amounts of food.

GERMINATE – to begin to grow from a seed.

HERB – a scented plant used to flavor food or make medicine.

MATURE – to finish growing or developing.

SANDWICH – two pieces of bread with a filling, such as meat, cheese, or peanut butter, between them.

SHAMPOO – a special soap used to clean hair.

SPROUT – 1. to begin to grow. 2. a new plant growing from a seed.

TRANSPORTATION – the act of moving people and things.

Web Sites

*To learn more about growing and cooking food, visit ABDO Publishing Company on the World Wide Web at **www.abdopublishing.com**. Web sites about creative ways for kids to grow and cook food are featured on our Book Links page. These links are routinely monitored and updated to provide the most current information available.*

Index